Don't Get Too High
(said the Bird to the Fly)

Written and Illustrated by Mic Fox

Please write Famly LLC at fortfamly.com

ISBN 9781974682386

for my Famly

The bird and the fly were both very good friends.
How good of friends?
Well, that sort of depends.

The fly was so loyal
but a bit of a jerk.

The bird was responsible
but addicted to work.

They were the best two friends that ever could be–
Went to the same college–same fraternity.

They were always together–
Day in and day out.

They had all sorts of fun.
That's what friendship's about.

The bird, he could soar
on the wind with his wings.

Then he'd find a nice branch,
and he'd sit there and sing.

The fly he could buzz.
He was a wonderful flyer.

He loved flying high
then getting higher and higher.

College was fun–
They both got their degrees.

They made a few friends–
Even more memories.

The bird met a girl
and moved back to the 'burbs.

But the fly loved the city
and moved in with a worm.

Still they promised to meet up
at least once a week–

Catch up, chew the fat,
get some food by the creek.

The week turned to a month
and a month into six.

The bird started a family–
Built a house out of sticks.

The fly missed the bird
and the good times in school.

He thought of them often.
He thought they were cool.

The bird wasn't around
as much
anymore.

The fly found the bird's new life
to be
a bore.

But they finally met up
on a Thursday in May–
At the park by the fly's house
where they used to play.

The bird came from work
and was there right on time.

But the fly showed up late,
a little out of his mind.

The bird said,
"Hey fly!
It's been way too long.
My wife says, 'Hello.'
Sends her best, with a song."

"Oh yeah?" said the fly,
"Tell her that I said, 'Hey.'
What do you want to do
for the rest of the day?"

"We could grab us a drink."
said the bird with a grin.

"Or we could get high
like we used to, my friend."

"Ha!" said the bird,
"I haven't flown in a minute.
You still fly all the time?
Like... you're still sorta in it?"

"Of course," said the fly,
"I'm high most every night.
Wanna give it a shot?"

"Hey!" said the fly,
"What happened to you?
I'm going up anyway.
What're you gonna do?"

"No–I think I'm all right."

"Well, don't get too high."
said the bird to the fly.

But the fly replied,
"Why?
What if I like getting high?"

And the bird said,

"The last time that you got too high,
you ignored all your friends
while you were up in the sky.

You ate all the food
and you were in a weird mood.
Then you talked about
nonsensical philosophy, dude.

I don't mind getting high on occasion, it's fun.
But now I've got a kid and a business to run.

So if you want to get high sometimes,
it's fine by me...........

But too high is too high,
and that's too high, you see?"

"Too high to see what?
I don't see where you're going.
I'm a little high now."

"I can see that. It's showing.

There's a difference
between flying
and getting too high.
I mean,
you know the difference.
You're a smart guy."

"Getting high
doesn't make me lazy,
you know."

"But it's one thing to say so,
another to show."

"Hey!
I'm still a contributing
member of society.
I walk down the street
and people say 'Hi' to me.

I get high before work
and still get my work done.
I fly whenever I want
and have plenty of fun.

Getting high doesn't make me who I am.
It's not all that I do. Listen, you have a fam.
And your family's the most important thing in your life.
But I don't have a family and I think that's all right."

"But you have me, fly."
said the bird with compassion.

"But you're never around."
the fly's instant reaction.

"Maybe I'd be around
if you weren't high everyday."

"Maybe I would come down,
if you called up to say 'Hey.'"

"Well, man" said the bird,
"Never heard it like that.
I should give you a call.
Maybe see where you're at."

"And I should call too.
I miss the old days, you know?"

"But time passes on
and we continue to grow."

"You've gotta get out
of your routine, fly.
There's so much of the world
that you miss when you're high.

You've got friends who love you.
You do what you do.
But they'll keep living their lives
with or without you."

The fly replied,
"My, well,
that would just be a shame.
And I guess, well,
our friendship
would not be the same.

And I'd miss all the fun times
down here on the ground.
So I won't get too high
and I'll stick around."

And you wouldn't believe it, but there, in the end,
the bird and the fly became friends again.

They'd call on each other if they were feeling blue.
And they'd meet up on the weekends and hit the barbecue.

They promised to be better–to be more understanding.
And they promised to be friendlier–to not be so demanding.

And on occasion, they'd meet up for drinks and games and stuff.
Then they'd fly off into the sky and get just high enough.

28319238R00019

Made in the USA
Lexington, KY
12 January 2019